AF449265

A Diary of Personal Prayer

By Julie Jensen McDonald

Photography by Joan Liffring-Zug
Calligraphy by Esther Feske
Cover design by Mike Crilley
Edited by John Zug, David Duer, Scott Elledge and Valerie Staats.
Printed by Julin Printing Company, Monticello, Iowa
Typesetting: The Typesetting Connection, Iowa City, Iowa

Books by Mail: (postpaid)
All by Julie Jensen McDonald

A Diary of Personal Prayer
softbound $ 10.50
hardbound   18.50

Table Prayers: Good Graces
softbound $ 8.50
hardbound   18.50

Scandinavian Proverbs
softbound $ 7.50
hardbound   18.50

Delectably Danish: Recipes and Reflections
softbound $ 6.50
2 for   12.00
3 for   16.00

1986 prices subject to change.
For a complete list
of our books, write to:

Penfield Press
215 Brown Street
Iowa City, Iowa 52240

A Diary of Personal Prayer

© 1986 Julie Jensen McDonald
Photographs © 1986 Joan Liffring-Zug

Library of Congress Catalog Number 86-60689
ISBN 0-941016-34-X hardbound
ISBN 0-941016-35-8 softbound

ABOUT THE AUTHOR

Julie Jensen McDonald is the author of three Penfield Press titles: *Delectably Danish: Recipes and Reflections*, *Scandinavian Proverbs*, and *Good Graces*.

Her novels include *Amalie's Story*, *Petra*, and *The Sailing Out*, a trilogy about the lives of Danish women who came to America with their families, facing the hardships and victories of a new way of life.

Other books by Julie Jensen McDonald include *Ruth Buxton Sayre*, a biography; *The Ballad of Bishop Hill*, the story of a Swedish colony in Illinois; and *Baby Black*, a children's book.

Julie is a graduate of the University of Iowa, and holds an honorary Doctor of Letters degree from St. Ambrose College of Davenport, Iowa, where she teaches journalism. She is a visiting writer in the Artists-in-the-Schools program of the Iowa Arts Council. She has been women's editor, feature writer and art critic for daily newspapers. Her many awards include Quad-City Writer of the Year, Governor's Media in the Arts Award, and Johnson Brigham Award of the Iowa Library Association.

Julie Jensen McDonald is a woman of strong faith in the future, based on her own studies of the roles of both women and men in the unfolding of history and religion. Her writing is delightful and clear, filled with exceptional insight.

She is married to an attorney and is the mother of a son and a daughter.

CONTENTS

PREFACE

While searching for another piece of writing in a disorderly file cabinet, I came upon a sheaf of prayers I wrote for my own sake a long time ago and all but forgot.

As I reread the first few, the form seemed brash —as if I were explaining things to the Omniscient Creator, but then I realized that He would understand. I believe He was willing to listen while I tried to order my existence by reviewing my experiences.

I am a different person now than I was then, but I recognize a younger self and have a strong sense of God's shepherding care from that time to this. He heard my cries from the heart and patiently upheld me in the compelling concerns that He knew would work themselves out.

Looking back on my crooked road, I am more grateful than ever for my Divine traveling companion.

—Julie Jensen McDonald

PRAYER FOR WHOLENESS

Lord, many of Your creatures have a life work that engages them fully, and they enjoy a fairly unified existence, but You have made me in such a way that I climb on a horse and ride off in all directions.

While I thank You for the unfailing interest of such a condition, I pray that You will make me whole. Mesh my newspaper work with my journalism teaching. Keep me from letting fiction and fact contaminate each other. Help me to be fully present with my family and maintain a house that gives them comfort. Give me the strength and the skill to serve You in and out of the church, and help me remember to play so I won't grow sour and weary, becoming an ungrateful vessel for Your many blessings. Take the bright bits of my life and make a mosaic, Lord, for without You they are meaningless shards of glass. Amen.

PRAYER FOR
A NEW YEAR

Father, we drove into the country to see the old year out with friends. They are relatively new friends of ours, but they kindly took us into their circle of long and mellow relationships.

The night was crisp, cold and moonlit, and their house on a high hill was a warm haven of good fellowship and good food. As midnight struck, husbands and wives kissed with quiet affection in a salute to one more good year together. I thought of other times and other places where I had seen strangers in hectic and meaningless embraces as the old year passed, and I was thankful for this more seemly celebration.

And now, safe in bed, I pray for the safety of those who are drinking too much and driving too fast this night. I pray for those who cannot lay down the burden of the past and for those who fear the future.

I thank You for the blessings of the old year and for the pain that brought growth. You alone possess the full map of my life's journey, and I pray that You will keep me on the right road. Never let me forget that in You I live and move and have my being. Amen.

PRAYER FOR
A TRAVELER

Lord, our son left for Europe today, and we won't see him again for more than four months. Watch over him, I pray, because we cannot, and we are thankful that we can entrust him to You.

He and his friend looked young and vulnerable in their blue jeans and down jackets with back packs slung over their shoulders. They are trustful American kids, and I pray that You will guide them through situations where their trust might be misplaced.

When the flight was called, this gruff boy who has scorned visible displays of affection for years allowed me one farewell hug. He is all bones and sinew—and so tall. Oh Lord, protect this flesh of my flesh.

"Say good-bye to Dad and the dogs for me," he said, and then they went through the gate, two tall young men with a zest for discovery, nerved up for a great adventure and probably more apprehensive about the unknown than they wanted us to guess.

I thank You for the opportunity they have to stretch their experience. Go with them, Lord, and keep them in Your care. Amen.

PRAYER FOR A YOUNG COUPLE

Father, our former minister's son was married last night, and I pray that You will bless this union. They are so young, and yet they know their own hearts. They have joined their lives with sweet seriousness.

The bridegroom's high-school-age brother was a member of the wedding party, and he fainted twice during the ceremony, but dear Carl, the father, did not falter in the age-old words that make one life of two. His loving dignity made everything all right.

When the young couple had flown off to Puerto Rico, our old friends came to supper, and we realized the blessedness of the tie that binds our hearts in Christian love. The years we had been apart melted, and so did any disagreements we had had in times past.

As we drank in the solid goodness of this family seated around our table, I stopped worrying about the youth of the bridegroom. David and his wife will give You first place in their lives, Lord, and one cannot ask a better basis for a marriage than that. With high hopes for their happiness, I thank You. Amen.

PRAYER FOR A BLIND MUSICIAN

Father, I'm on tour with the college band. I haven't played three concerts a day since I was in college myself, and I thank You for the strength to do it.

Our guest soloist, Roy, has made all of us ashamed of minor complaints. Long ago, he worked through the rage and grief of losing his sight, and what remains is a humorous ruefulness at the nuisance of being blind.

What a marvel he is, making a beautiful concert instrument of the saxophone, which many consider to be a low-down horn. He reminds us that the common can be elevated by love and painstaking care.

Roy must memorize all his music by braille, by tape, or by having his wife describe the notation, and he is more attentive to the markings than those of us who can see.

His wife is pregnant with their third child, he doesn't have a real job, and he lives in a world of perpetual darkness in a body fragilely dependent on insulin balance. Yet Roy has hope. Forgive me for bearing the insignificant vicissitudes of my life with less grace.

Take care of him, Father, and give him rich satisfaction in his life and in his art. Amen.

PRAYER OF THANKFULNESS

Dear Father, we have just learned that our son was robbed of his passport, traveler's checks, and Eurorail pass in Germany. My heart aches for him in this disheartening experience that I can do nothing about, but I thank You that he has the self-reliance to deal with it. He didn't call home and cry for help. We only know because his friend called home and mentioned it.

We have put him in Your care, Father, and we must and do believe that "all things work together for good" in his life away from us. Somehow this painful situation will produce growth.

We have had a letter from my Danish cousins saying that he is "a fine fellow". They know of his trouble, because it happened just before he came to them, but with the kind impulse to spare us worry, they said nothing about it. Bless them for that, Father.

Again, I commit him to You, and I thank You for his growing independence. Amen.

PRAYER FOR A NEW SEMESTER

Lord, I met a new class this morning, and yet it isn't really new. Most of the students were with me last semester, and those who were not must justify their readiness for an advanced course. Two of them left immediately. I signed drop slips with multiple carbons, and that always gives me a sense of loss.

This time, I have only myself to blame if they are not prepared for the course work—except for the pretty girl who took a journalism course at another college and the boy who worked on a newspaper somewhere. What an affection I feel for them all! The longer I teach, the more of my heart I surrender to the students. Keep me from spoiling them with maternal fondness, Father.

I pray Your blessing on this lovely, manageable class of eleven. Open their minds and give them confidence, for we have much to do.

Help me to challenge but not to overburden, to criticize kindly, and to praise when praise is due. I am mindful of my tendency to take excellence for granted, Lord. Give me the empathy that sees it as a new triumph and let me celebrate it as such. Amen.

PRAYER FOR RESOLVE

Father, I have decided to put my newspaper series of fifty town histories into book form, and the newspaper is giving me the rights. However, my editor, who promised to save the computer tapes of the stories, has thrown them away. This means I will have to type a hundred and fifty thousand words back into the electronic system, and I quail at the prospect.

First of all, I do not know how to operate the terminal, but I do thank You for my friend John, who spent an evening showing me the procedure and who has promised to help.

Father, help me not to despair at the magnitude of the task and the time it will take. At first, I thought You were telling me not to make the book, but as I thought and prayed about it, it came to me that so much history should not be lost.

Also, it will be some kind of a victory to conquer the electronic system. I am still uncertain and afraid when the words "incorrect command" flash on the terminal screen, but if You put it into the mind of man to devise this system, surely You will give me the understanding I need to make use of it. This is my prayer, and I thank You even as I ask it. Amen.

PRAYER FOR MY BIBLE TEACHER

Lord, I am so thankful for Your servant George, who teaches the non-denominational Bible class I attend every Monday night.

You have brought him back from the edge of death in a way that baffles medical doctors, and though his body is frail, his spirit is a flame that warms nearly a hundred hearts on that special night each week.

The big room in the YWCA fills with teens, old people, young married couples, and the middle-aged—Catholics, Protestants, and Jews. We come because we are hungry for an understanding of Your Word, and we are filled by Pastor George's deep and careful exposition of it, verse by verse.

In spite of sickness and difficulty, both Pastor George and his wife radiate joy. They love us all without a trace of sentimentality, weeping when we weep and rejoicing when we rejoice.

Truly, Lord, they are thankful in all things. Bless them, keep them, and let them continue in their joyous service. Thank You for their work and for their lives. Amen.

BIRTHDAY PRAYER

Father, I thank You for this man, my husband, who was born on this day. He has been mine more than half his life, and I am grateful for our years together.

He was a premature baby, a sickly child, and he nearly died of peritonitis in his high school years, but You saved him for me.

He seems to be a tough lawyer, Father, but his heart is tender. When we had dinner guests the other night, a client telephoned, ranting that he would kill his wife and then himself. Jack excused himself from the table and talked to the man for more than half an hour, calming him down, and came back to say, "He just needed someone to listen to him."

And he gave me my valentine early, a pair of fleece-lined gloves to keep the chill of winter from an arthritic wrist.

While he complains about man-made "theological Mickey Mouse," Lord, he does love You and Your Son. Bless him in his new year and hold him close. Amen.

PRAYER OF SUBMISSION

Lord, I drove out to the highway this morning, trying to keep an interview appointment in another town, and I turned back because I was afraid. The snow was blowing and drifting, and the road was slippery. I'm thankful to be home and warm and alive.

This is a hard winter, Lord. People are freezing to great discomfort, if not to death, and some are without water and food. Your natural world can be cruel, Lord.

On the television news tonight I saw a report from a medical researcher saying that a cure for cancer would not be found in our lifetime or any lifetime. Can that be so, Lord? I can only believe that You are telling us once more, "The arm of flesh will fail you, you dare not trust your own."

I submit, Lord, putting myself in Your Omnipotent, Omniscient, Omnipresent care. Without You, I would die of sheer terror in this age of doomsday planes, cancer-producing environments, and senseless evil. Despite the way things seem, You are Lord of all and in complete control. Amen.

HIGHWAY PRAYER

Lord, it is so beautiful as I drive into a part of my state I have never seen before. The fields are tawny here in the south where there is no snow, and the road curves between rounded hills.

The counties have lovely names like Poweshiek and Mahaska. The only false note is a motel called the King Lear outside a neat, Dutch town with Delft tiles set into the bandstand in the city square.

I am to be Writer-in-the-Schools in a town of a thousand where they have never had a visiting artist before. They probably are afraid of me, Lord, and I am afraid that I may bring them less than they expect. Reassure them and me, I pray.

So much pain goes with being a writer that I wonder if it's right to get young people excited about it. Only if I tell the bad things too, I suppose. There's a glory in trying. Lord, be with me through this week. Amen.

PRAYER OF JOY

Father, how good it is to feel admiration and response! I wasn't sure I could work with kindergartners, but I tried today, and they came close while I read them a story, touching me as softly as moths. They can't write yet, but they make beautiful associations for someone else to write down: "The stars fell down and made ice on the sidewalk."

The older kids look at me with eyes that are alive and accept new possibilities for themselves. They are country children with a deep love for the land. My coordinator, the art teacher, is working to help her husband buy a farm, and her art is rooted in all that's real.

Because there is no motel here, I live in a town twenty miles away, and the people there are curious about the stranger who eats alone reading a book titled *The Tabernacle.* Father, how did I get this old without knowing the deep meaning of your specific orders for the building of that holy place? Oh God, my Father, You are random in nothing.

I pray Your blessing on all the students and teachers I have come to love so soon, especially Sally, a fine writer who sees no college in her future. Give her what is best. Amen.

PRAYER ON COMING HOME

Lord, thank You for bringing me safely back. My pink hyacinths have shriveled in their pot, a week's mail is piled on the dining room table, and my cat is scolding me for abandoning him. The dogs greet me with some enthusiasm, and my husband obviously has tried to pick up the house before going to the office.

Once more I must buy groceries, cook, clean, and do the laundry, but I have had my respite from dailiness, and I can do these things gladly for awhile.

I'm eager to see how my students fared with the substitutes and to throw myself into newspaper assignments. And here's a note—our son phoned from Barcelona and is well.

As I dig into the mail, there is a letter from a publisher in response to my query: "Please send the manuscript." My cup runneth over!

But there's more. Jack is just driving into the garage, and how I've missed him! Amen.

A PRAYER OF UPROOTING

Father, I have been digging up dandelions for hours. Yesterday I dug three grocery sacks full of them, and when I got up this morning, the lawn was just as thickly sprinkled with sassy, yellow faces as it ever had been.

My hands ache, my legs are stiff, and my nails are dirty and broken. To what purpose? I work like this to keep from being a bad neighbor, because *I* love the color of dandelion blossoms and admire the sunray arrangement of the jagged leaves. The artful scattering of the yellow blooms against the green grass makes a pattern that pleases my eye. The neighbors, however, prefer solid green, and my dandelion seeds in their fluffy parachutes have no respect for lot lines. I must give up my floral gold to keep from imposing it on others.

When I was a child, we were poor enough to eat dandelion greens, and they tasted like bitter spinach. I thank You that I need not eat them now.

And so I dig on. If I do this day after day, will they finally be gone? Or will they, like my sins and shortcomings, crop up again and again? As I attack these bright weeds that I love, I wonder just how much I love my sins. Wither that love, Father, and help me to uproot the blooms of wickedness, not for the sake of the neighbors, but for Christ, whose sacrifice covers my guilt. Amen.

PRAYER OF HOPE

Father, my husband has a chance to be a district judge, as You know. The Bar Association voted that his name and that of a woman lawyer be submitted to the judicial nominating committee, along with three others. He and the woman survived that committee, and now the matter rests with the governor.

He wants it very much, Father, and he would be a good man on the bench. He's fair, honest, thorough, and hard-working. He's also in love with the ideal of Justice. However, these days women have the edge, and I suppose it's about time. The battle against discrimination always seems to call for a time of transition when qualifications must be sacrificed to the redress of old wrongs. Of course, the woman may be well qualified, too.

My friends, the nuns, are "praying that he'll get it". Pastor George, however, says that he and his wife are "praying that he'll get it if it's God's will". I'll pray with George and Lynda, Father, because who could want something against Your will? You know what is best and can see beyond our limited field of vision.

If the governor appoints him to the bench, we'll have less money than he would make in private practice, but that doesn't matter. I want him to do what would make him happy because I love him. And I would like him spared the dull ache of disappointment. So if it's Your will, Father, put him in a judge's robe. If not, help me comfort him. Amen.

COMMENCEMENT PRAYER

Father, I always enjoy wearing the beautiful satin and velvet stole I received with my honorary Doctor of Letters degree in an academic procession. I didn't work for mine in the usual way, which makes me appreciate the hard-won adornments of my colleagues even more—hours and years of study made visible in this rainbow of laurels. I know that these people can be petty and difficult, but how grand they are on commencement day!

I had no special emotional investment in this graduating class, but I looked into each face with generalized affection as the student procession passed. They are uncertain but eager, relieved to be done with this phase of their lives but nervous about what comes next.

A United States senator, looking like an ancient Roman in his academic gown, counseled them to take chances while they are young enough to afford mistakes. This wasn't what they expected to hear, and they might have been more comfortable with "the usual junk". What he said made me believe that even I can still take chances. Because I'm safe in Your hands, it's never too late to commence.

Be with them, Father, and with me too. Amen.

PRAYER FOR NEW FRIENDS

Dear Lord, I thank You for Marian, who took me into her home while I worked as Writer-in-the-Schools in her town. Widowed young, she has reared a large family on her own, and if her adult children are as fine as the high school senior I came to know, she has done admirable double duty as a parent.

We talked late into the night, sharing things we have read, thought, and experienced, knowing there would be no time for a long, gradual period of getting acquainted. Sometimes her daughter Jill would join us at the kitchen table with a glass of iced tea, bringing that special sense of life bursting into bloom as she spoke of her graduation-present trip, college, and the unformed shimmer of her more distant future.

Marian has taken great pains to know herself. She keeps detailed journals that chart her living and help her find more perfect patterns, and she knows the value of quiet reflection. I cannot be like her, but I am enriched by our meeting.

Thank You for Marian and Jill, Lord. Be very near to them. Amen.

PRAYER OF ACCEPTANCE

Well, Lord, my husband isn't going to be a judge. Not soon, anyhow. I remind myself that I must accept this as an answer to prayer.

I knew before the paper came tonight. An aide in the governor's office called here to ask for him, though he was closer to them than to me—in the state capital on business. I wish I were with him to absorb the disappointment.

I know he's trying to find the new judge to congratulate her, and that he will be gracious in spite of the metallic taste of loss.

Shall I build a careful edifice of reasons? Harvest a crop of sour grapes? No, not even if his clients do need him and the family firm will go on, possibly to the third generation. Not even if he can make more money before the bar than on the bench.

How devious I am, Lord! Forgive me for needing human reasons for events that are in Your hands. Make him too busy to nurse regret, and keep us both where You want us. Amen.

VACATION PRAYER

Father, I thank You for the two safe flights that have brought us to Kennedy airport, and now as we settle in the big Finnair plane, I pray once more for our safety.

At the beginning of a trip, I always feel that I have barely escaped with my life from the hectic dailiness at home; that my familiar world can't possibly manage without me. Were the instructions I left explicit enough? Will the delivery of milk and newspapers really stop? Help me to leave all that behind.

The man beside me has been my husband for years, but when we're not traveling, I talk to strangers more than I do to him, questioning them with bright (and real) interest for my newspaper stories. Now my husband and I will be together night and day for more than three weeks, and we have by no means come to the end of new things to learn about each other. May we offer each other the best. Just now, we're tired, and we hold hands wordlessly.

We call this a vacation, the English call it a holiday, and the Russians call it a rest. Father, let it be all three for us. Amen.

PRAYER IN A FINNISH CHURCH

Lord, You are everywhere, but I feel Your presence most strongly today in the beautiful Temppeliaukio church sunk into the rocks in Helsinki. The copper near the skylight gleams like the fiery tongues of Pentecost, and the daylight enters softly.

"On this rock I will build my church." Deep *in* the rocks, this church dramatizes the verse for me. How safe it seems here.

Chattering tourists fall silent when they enter, and when it's time for our group to leave, I linger, looking back. I want to take the safety with me, and so I can, for God does not dwell exclusively in houses made with hands.

Preserve this sanctuary in my memory, Lord, and let me return to it when I am hard-pressed. Amen.

PRAYER IN
AN ALIEN LAND

Father, every inch of our suitcases was searched as we entered the Soviet Union at Tallinn, Estonia. The customs official pulled out my battered Bible, looked at it with a frown, and called another man over for a conference. One is permitted to bring a Bible for personal use, but if they had confiscated it, I would not have complained. The Soviets sometimes read the things they take from people.

After dinner at our hotel, we walked to the rooms of the English Club in the old city and talked with two Soviet Estonians who wanted to practice our language: Martin, whose wife died last spring and whose thirteen-year-old daughter misses her mother; and Illmar, who is interested in the language of the Hopi Indians. They are very much like us in every way but one: they do not acknowledge You.

I did not speak out, Father, because we were together less than two hours. It takes more time to find the right moment. I do pray that the moment will come for them somewhere, with someone. I beseech You not to limit their opportunity to the moment I missed. Amen.

PRAYER ON
RED SQUARE

Father, we're in Moscow briefly on our way to Odessa, and as we walked past the tomb of Lenin in a cold drizzle, we saw a bride in her wedding dress waiting to pay her respects to the only real Soviet deity.

Lenin definitely is not risen. The only question is whether he's wax. An English-speaking diplomat confided to us that they call him "Dead Fred".

The Russians are a reverent people, displaying deep feeling in the presence of their objects of worship. I would be the first to agree that "religion is the opiate of the people," but faith is something else; faith in a Person whose remains cannot be visited.

We paid thirty kopecks apiece to enter St. Basil's cathedral with its bright, fairy-tale domes. A different kind of reverence can be found there, in spite of a stench many centuries old. I want to believe that a beautiful icon of Christ still stirs something in the Russian heart. Father, fan that tiny flame. Amen.

PRAYER IN ODESSA

Lord, the Black Sea doesn't look very black, but it's cold! I waded into it with a Catholic priest and bit my lips in pain.

We went to what was billed as a ballet performance at the opulent Viennese opera house, and it turned out to be a new modern opera plus a one-act ballet. We couldn't understand much of the opera, but the theme was war and the immortality gained by dying for Mother Russia. The audience didn't like the opera much, but flowers rained at the dancers' feet.

Jack bought me a gold ring set with an imitation ruby, the kind of thing Russian women seem to love. I think of the virtuous woman of Scripture whose "price is above rubies," confident that mine is above *this* ruby.

Our highest experience in Odessa was the Russian Orthodox church service this morning. Large, leafy tree branches decorated the walls of the church; the floor was thickly covered with rushes, and the worshippers stood while the service was chanted and beautiful voices sounded from a choir balcony. Looking into the high dome, we saw the face of Christ in a magnificent icon. The sight of Him was pure joy. Amen.

PRAYER IN THE STEPPES

"There's a wideness in God's mercy." This line from a hymn went through my mind as I looked out across the steppes and saw no boundary but horizon.

This vast expanse seems to engender largeness of heart in the people who live on it. We stopped at a small wayside restaurant and were served an elegant meal of many courses at tables decorated with American flags. As we left, the waitresses came after us with broad smiles, offering roses from the tables.

We were the first large delegation of foreign visitors at a state farm, and the children met us with more flowers. Their elders offered cold mineral water, handshakes, and kisses.

All Russians do not hate all Americans. Thank You for the wideness of Your reality, Lord. Amen.

PRAYER FOR FRIENDSHIP

Lord, a dozen invited Soviet guests are aboard the Alexander Pushkin, and tonight on the top deck they sat behind a table facing us across a wide gulf of space. Help us to narrow the distance.

Among them are a family of three, Sergei and Natasha and their small daughter Masha, a beautiful girl named Alma, a middle-aged professor, a seaman from Murmansk, Yuri from Leningrad, two young men from Novgorod, and Tia from Estonia.

Tonight they were formal and wary. We are inclined to be more outgoing, but we didn't want to spook them.

The professor said in a joking manner, "You will be asking us for Communist Party cards by the end of the cruise." We laughed politely. Their accomplishments in the six decades since the Revolution are impressive, but they have been costly in human terms.

I did speak to Tia about how difficult it was for me to conceive of a godless society. She looked around nervously and said in a low voice, "There will always be some faith. They can't get rid of it all." Then she quickly excused herself.

Nourish that faith, Lord, wherever it is. Amen.

PRAYER ON KOSSACK'S ISLAND

Father, we anchored at a beautiful green island in the Don today, and Jack went ashore early to bring me a wild rose.

He was on the volleyball team against a Soviet team, and they tried to let us win to be polite, but they simply couldn't play that poorly.

Talking with some Americans on the beach, we decided they were nearly ready to ask for their Communist Party cards. They cited the lack of juvenile delinquency, unemployment, and energy crises in the Soviet Union as plusses for their system of government.

Our government works more the way You do, Father, or so it seems to me. You created man with free will, and bad choices make him suffer, but You do not force good choices. There is precious little free choice in the U.S.S.R., and I would not trade what we have for any amount of social good and no options.

As it grew dark, we all carried wood to a friendship fire and tried to join in Russian songs and dances. On that ground, we can meet. Help us to multiply our possibilities of meeting. Amen.

PRAYER FOR TAMARA

Lord, today on the beach I talked with the beautiful Intourist guide, Tamara, the one who everyone says doesn't look Russian because she has such chic. I had smiled and said "hello" to her frequently before, but she never encouraged conversation. I guess it's different out in the open, where you can see whether anyone is listening.

Tamara, who looks like an American teenager, is divorced and has a son of school age, which means he must be at least seven. After her formal schooling, she was trained and certified to sew in a children's clothing factory, but she longed for more and went to Moscow University to study English and American literature.

This, of course, has brought her into conflict with her own society. She knows there are other ways of life, and she wants what she can't have. We talked about books. I gave her Ken Kesey, and she gave me Lermontov. We were sorry to part when it was lunch time.

The next time we met aboard the Alexander Pushkin, I greeted her warmly, and she answered without a smile, with no light in her eyes. Oh Lord, let her be free. Amen.

PRAYER IN LENIN'S HOMETOWN

Father, today we came to Ulyanovsk, the town where Lenin was born. On a quiet, tree-lined street of houses decorated with carved wood, we visited one of the many homes where he lived.

Strangely, it was a house of great peace, not at all what one would expect from a seedbed of revolution. Lenin's mother made it so, creating a safe and comfortable nest for the many children she reared alone while their father was away supervising education in the region.

The guide told us how she traveled great distances to be with her sons when they were in trouble, when they were in exile. And she was forever moving from one house or apartment to another.

Here in this cool, thick-walled house of pale rooms with heavy, expensive furniture I thought how she must have grieved when her son Alexander was hanged for an attempt on the life of the czar. The aftermath was the shaming of a younger son as the brother of a culprit—shame that ended in revolution. What could she have done to make things otherwise? You alone can know. Amen.

A PRAYER ON CREATING

Lord, while we were anchored at Kazan, the ancient capital of Genghis Khan, a group of composers, musicians, and writers of the Tatar Republic came aboard to perform and speak with us through interpreters.

The most moving pieces they performed were the ancient Tatar love songs. The yearning melodies depended little on the words to carry their meaning. A contemporary composition by one of the men sounded suspiciously like Gershwin.

The novelist was a member of the Writers' Union and recently had published a novel about the oil workers that sold one hundred thousand copies in fifteen days.

The Peoples' Artists are paid a salary like all other workers in the U.S.S.R., and while they are spared from total risk, they also are denied any real hope of glory. Their creations must serve the state, and this end seems to satisfy them.

You know how often I pray to be published and read, but if this cannot be granted, give me the grace to fail without complaint. Amen.

MOSCOW PRAYER

Father, we're back on Gorky Street, turning the corner to walk long blocks to the Pushkin Museum with its room full of Matisses and huge, pastel Bonnards. These artists were not on salary!

Walking through GUM, the huge department store along Red Square, we looked at high-priced merchandise we couldn't imagine anyone wanting. The Russians do want it, and the minute a new shipment of anything comes in, no matter how atrocious, they cluster around it in high excitement.

Once more we visited the Armory museum in the Kremlin, marveling at the carriages of the czars and the opulent gowns of the czarinas, reflecting on a time of unimaginable luxury for the few and unimaginable suffering for the many. And yet, the correction brought more suffering for all.

At the New Maiden convent, where the czars imprisoned their cast-off wives, we saw a painter working at his easel and bought a tempera landscape for ten rubles. When we asked him to sign it, he hesitated, and I suspect he signed a false name.

This city seems filled with suspicion and raw power, yet Tanya, one of our guides, says she couldn't live anywhere else.

Once there were crosses on the Kremlin towers. Will they stand against the sky again? Amen.

PRAYER FOR PEACE

We're in Leningrad, Lord, the city that endured nine hundred days of siege in World War II.

"It's too beautiful to live in," Tanya says. "A museum."

Instead of a city tour, which we had done before, we booked a trip to Pushkin Village on our own and visited the summer palace Peter the Great built for Catherine I. Their daughter Elizabeth made it grander in the Rastrelli manner. The Nazis ruined it completely, and carefully-trained practitioners of ancient crafts have restored it to what it was—except for the slabs of amber on the walls of one room. They were hidden and never have been found.

An army band played Viennese waltzes as we walked through the formal gardens with lilacs in bloom: the illusion of an idyllic past was complete, and it made us strangely uneasy.

Thank You, Lord, for putting the past behind us. If it were to come again, the good things might be flawed, and the bad things might be even more terrible.

We talked with survivors of the siege who said, "We must have peace! You can't know what war is!" Give them rest from their past, Lord, and give us all the wisdom to seek peace. Amen.

PRAYER FOR OUR SOVIET FRIENDS

Father, we said good-bye to our guides at the railroad station tonight, giving them flowers and small gifts. They waved, wistfully, it seemed, as their figures grew small in the distance.

The train was searched thoroughly by border guards to be sure that none of the guides accepted our invitation to come along. Watching a man in uniform lift the corridor rug to look under it, I was thankful that I could be amused rather than frightened by the thorough search.

The conductress would not open the windows on the hot train because she had heard that Americans threw mattresses out the windows. We tried to correct that impression to no avail and were forced to swelter.

At last we were in comfortable, unrestricted Finland, and we thought of the friends we had left behind. Several of the guides would have a short rest, but others had to report for work the next day, taking on a new group of tourists. Would they remember us?

Take care of them, Father. And take care of Martin and Ilmar and Yuri and Tia. Amen.

PRAYER FOR RELIEF

Father, I'm sweltering! Last night the central air-conditioning stopped working, and at the highest temperature of the summer. I can't go someplace cool because I'm waiting for a repairman who may or may not come.

It shames me to think how dependent I am on mechanical devices. My Bible reading today was in the Book of Job, and that shamed me even more, but I'm still obsessed by my own minor suffering.

I've tried every device remembered from childhood: pulling shades, opening and closing windows, drinking iced tea. I'm working myself into a sweat trying to get cool—or cooler.

If You can put it in the repairman's heart to hurry, I'll be grateful, but in the meantime, let me find that unchanging internal weather of Your presence; that atmosphere in which I live and move and have my being unmindful of thermometers. Amen.

PAINTER'S PRAYER

Lord, I thought I might get by with just washing the kitchen walls, but I can't. No cleanser will remove all the marks of broiler smoke from countless Sunday steaks or the scars from an exploding pressure cooker.

The painting goes so slowly with windows and corners, and as hard as I try to obliterate them, brush marks show.

The man from the home improvement company came to measure for a replacement window (one I won't have to paint) and said, "You're crazy to do this yourself! Can't you afford to have it done?"

Of course I can, but I'd rather make a mess myself than watch somebody else do it. Besides, painters never come when they say they will, chaining you to the house while you wait for them.

I'm making the walls yellow again, the color of the light in which You dwell, I like to think. When I'm finished, the job won't be perfect. I'll always know where the shadows are, but I'll say, "At least it's clean."

When Christ makes all things new, there are no brush marks, no shadows, and the job never has to be done again. Thank You, God, for that. Amen.

PRAYER OF ANXIETY

Father, when I went down to read proofs today, they told me how much my history book would actually cost, and I was terrified! Will I ever sell enough to break even?

You know all the brave noises I've been making about my willingness to take a loss in the interests of history, and You also know that I realized the possible amount of loss intellectually but not emotionally. Estimates aren't as frightening as accounts payable.

I keep thinking of all the other things both of us could do with that money: travel, improve our home, give to good causes. I now have a better understanding of why publishers are so chary of taking on a manuscript.

Oh God, I can't really see the future of the book, but You gave me the confidence to begin, and I pray that You will give me the confidence to see it through. Amen.

PRAYER OF RELIEF

Lord, hold the air-conditioning repair man in the hollow of Your hand! It seemed a year until he came, but now that I'm cool again, I realize that he made uncommon haste.

I have been insufficiently thankful for the many comforts of my life: an indoor atmosphere tempered to the season, hot water, indoor plumbing (I do remember the other kind), and machines to perform much of my labor. Today I'm numbering them all like pearls in a necklace.

I'm thinking too of those who for one reason or another go unsheltered from the elements, who walk great distances for water, and who have no tools but their own tired bodies. Please let them know the gladness of relief I now enjoy. Amen.

PRAYER OF CHANGE

Father, our son helped rearrange our bedroom furniture today, the first big change in twenty-three years. I suspect that some of the dust beneath the heaviest pieces was nearly a quarter of a century old.

For so many years I've said my nightly prayers with my eyes fixed on the cross formed by ceiling beams in the dim light that filters through the curtains, and now I can't see it. I was upset until I reminded myself that no visual image can hold the perfection of the Three-in-One.

My husband tosses restlessly, and when I say, "Can't you sleep upside down?", he says, "The light is different." So it is, and we are such creatures of habit that difference upsets us mightily.

I'm so thankful that You are the same yesterday, today, and tomorrow—without shadow of turning. All other change becomes unimportant in the light of that precious truth. Amen.

PRAYER ON
THE DEATH OF A COUSIN

Father, it was kind of You to take Bill home so gently. It lessens our grief. He was a musician, a composer, and a conductor, and he could not have asked for a better finale. Full of years and honors, he stepped off the rehearsal podium into a peaceful death.

I hadn't seen him for decades, and a bad case of bronchitis kept me from driving across the state to his funeral. You and I both know that I *could* have gone, but why should I disrupt the dignity of the services with a hacking cough?

My mother wrote to give me the details. All the members of the Karl King Band came in uniform, and Bill's conductor's cap was on the coffin in place of a family wreath. The college where he taught suspended classes for the day.

A better memorial than my presence on that day, I thought, was to play well at our next band concert in the park. His instrument, the clarinet, is also mine, and I played my very best for Bill.

Thank You for his life and work, and I pray that You will comfort his family. Amen.

PRAYER AFTER
A PLAY

Lord, I have reviewed so many bad local theatrical productions that I feared for my discrimination. I'm thankful to know that excellence still sends a shiver up my spine.

Surely it's a gift from You when actors can take us out of ourselves completely, make us believe in the reality of their circumscribed stage.

When you know the ending of a play and still hope against hope that it will turn out better for the characters this time, then all the elements of great theater are working. How rare and wonderful it is!

The actors in this company work more for love than money, and they spend themselves without stint. They have much in common with practicing Christians, it occurs to me.

Help us all to live as ardently, and to polish our gifts, whatever they may be. Amen.

DESK-CLEANING PRAYER

Father, I have worked in utter chaos far too long. When piles of papers on my desk started to fall on me, I began to throw things away. It takes a long time, because I have to read and look at everything, forcing myself to throw when I'm inclined to keep.

Here's a letter I wrote to a friend and never mailed—two years old and not very significant. My friend missed very little. Here's one written to me by someone I can't remember—also not very significant. The pads of interview notes, kept for improbable reference, are climbing toward the ceiling. Out! A little piece I wrote titled "Puny Parables" catches my eye. Not bad, but I no longer understand all my references.

When six grocery bags are filled with papers I no longer need, I realize that I have been living on the run for years, never taking time to clean and order this magpie's nest. Is my mind in the same condition?

Lord, help me to discard thoughts and attitudes for which I have no earthly use. Give me a cleared working space within. Amen.

PRAYER DURING A PANEL DISCUSSION

Lord, I have made my initial statement, saying what I think I know about the state of the arts, and now I'm trying to listen to the others. I'm as bad as an Athenian, craving a new thing, and I'm not hearing it.

How impatient I get! But all these words strung together with varying degrees of grace have been said a thousand times before. Yet I see some people in the audience taking notes.

Ah, the discussion is open to the floor now, and a man is attacking my art reviews. He calls them "narrative," and I'm tempted to say that I seldom carry on dialogue with objects hanging on walls, but I refrain. It seems that he wants me to state whether the artist carried out his or her intention. How can I know? I can only report what I see and how it speaks to me.

We break for coffee, and most of the participants seem excited about the interchange. I'm not, because it won't change anything. We'll all go on groping in our own way for the good, the true, and the beautiful. Help us in our quest. Amen.

PRAYER OF REUNION

Father, a third of my high school class was reunited tonight, and we had such a warm and happy time thirty years after our graduation.

My old nickname, unused these thirty years, seemed strange to me, and it took me a while to respond to it. They gave me a copy of a poem I supposedly wrote, and I did not recognize it.

But I did remember faces and voices, essentially unchanged, and we all talked and reminisced with true affection. We are less critical now, and time has mellowed our youthful insecurities.

The class beauty has wrinkles like the finest lace from too much tropical sun. The fat, quiet girl is a champion of women's rights. The gauche farm boy is a suave agri-businessman. The boy who wore glasses with lenses like the bottoms of Coke bottles revels in the freedom of contact lenses. Only two of our number have been taken by death. You have dealt with us kindly, Father.

I wanted some new success to bring to this occasion as a trophy, but I had none, and they loved me just as well. Better, perhaps? Forgive that nasty thought, but You know human nature.

Bless our class and give each member of it gladness and peace. Amen.

PRAYER OF GRATITUDE

Lord, Lord, Lord, You have given me my heart's desire, and my heart, soul, and mind are taking off like rockets in bursts of joyful thanks! To have a novel accepted for publication after years of rejection seems too wonderful to be true, but the contract is right here in my hand.

It was so hard to wait, Lord, but maybe the waiting has made this miracle sweeter. Deep down, I know that Your time schedule is better than any I can hope to devise, but still I fuss and complain. Forgive me for that.

My self-confidence, which was getting tattered, is now restored, and it feels so good! Even so, I do not depend on my own strength or ability. You made me, and You loved me just as well the day before my book was accepted.

Lord, I know that no human is good. Only Christ attains that condition. However, it's easier to approach goodness when one is happy, and I am so grateful for this deep happiness. Amen.

PRAYER IN A REFORMATORY

Dear Father, tonight the State Training School for Girls is furnishing dormitory space for the Artists-in-the-Schools conference, and I wonder about the previous occupants of my room.

The door has no inside knob, and no one is threatening to lock me in, but I still feel panic as I scrabble on its surface with splayed hands to pull it open. It swings inward for me, but I visualize some unhappy child pulling and pounding on it to no avail.

Inside a drawer I find the letters h-e-l-l cut from a magazine and pasted to the wood, an apt description of what this room has been for some young girl. The rosy walls and the blond furniture held no warmth and light for her, because she was in a place of separation. That's hell, Father, being separated from You.

Please work in the lives of all the girls who have tossed on the bed where I now sit and wonder about them. The building is old enough for some of them to be mothers, even grandmothers, now. Whoever they are, wherever they may be, give them peace and fellowship with You.

I rise to scratch the "hell" out of the drawer, but then I leave it to speak its own harsh truth. Amen.

PRAYER OF FRUSTRATION

Lord, the rain that somebody prayed for came down in a rush and flooded the printing plant where my history book is being done. Nothing of mine was ruined, but my place in the schedule is lost. Again I must wait.

The promise of a textbook order flies away on dollar-bill wings, and I have visions of books under my bed and piled to my ears in every room—too many too late.

I want to rush to the plant with shovel and bucket to scoop mud, to get things on the move, but that's impossible. Instead, I pace and clench my fists. What a waste of force. Lord, please calm me down.

Help me to know that there is purpose in this circumstance, some good that loses no validity through my inability to recognize it.

I cannot bring myself to the Pollyanna state of seeing my flood as a drought-breaking blessing to someone else just yet, but as I pray, the fists unclench. Amen.

PRAYER FOR AN INANIMATE FRIEND

Father, I have to give up my car, and it is a sad parting. One of the young lawyers has left the firm, giving back a company car with fewer miles on it. I know it's sensible to make the change, but it's painful, too.

I never went so far as to call my car by name, but it was a comfortable extension of my body and responded valiantly to cold winter mornings and difficult terrain.

My newspaper ad brought scornful and indifferent seekers who muttered, "Gas hog!" (it isn't!), "That's a lot of miles" (happy miles), "It's really for my brother, and I'll have to talk to him" (he never will).

Offended, I patted the hood, thinking, "Never mind, old car, *I* appreciate you."

And then she came, a widow on a pension. She drove my car, loved it, and asked if I would sell for less. A good home is worth a lot, I thought, and I agreed.

Thank You for the good years and for the good miles, Father, and bless the buyer. The widow and the car seem right for each other. Both are still handsome with a lot of heart. And help me get used to the strange car that is now mine. Amen.

PRAYER FOR
MY MOTHER-IN-LAW

Lord, we've collected as much of our family as possible to picnic on this lovely bluff high above the Mississippi River and celebrate the birthday of my husband's mother.

She has changed very little in the many years I have known her. She still swims, bowls, and does more volunteer work than anyone I know. Today she is hiking through the woods on a broken toe without a word of complaint.

When I was a bride, her strength and asperity frightened me, and I remember so well how she shamed me out of crying at my own wedding.

By now, we have shared so many Christmases and so many everyday concerns that my awe has turned to deep affection. I admire the very qualities that scared me long ago. She has survived the death of parents, brothers, and husband, and she has strength for others in their need.

Never one for overt gestures of affection, she treats her grandchildren like adult friends, and because they have known her from their births, they understand.

I regret the time I wasted being afraid of this remarkable woman, Lord. Bless her on her birthday and give her more good years. Amen.

PRAYER FOR MY TONGUE

Dear Lord, at Bible study last night we talked about idle words, minced oaths, and casual profanity. When the discussion began, I felt quite superior, certain that I never took Your name in vain.

But all through this day I have been appalled at what comes out of my mouth. This morning when my college department head told me that I had failed to appear at an eight o'clock morning lecture that I thought was eight at night, I blurted, "My God!"

I banged my shin on the bed frame, and "Damn!" issued from my lips. A little later, I couldn't find my date book when someone wanted to make an appointment for next week, and a whispered "Hell!" escaped me. Forgive me, Lord.

I need the burning coal of Isaiah, though I can scarcely bear to read that verse. It's easy to rationalize that these private expletives do not reflect my true nature, that my heart is in the right place—but is it? Cleanse my heart, Lord, and my mouth will reflect its state. Amen.

PRAYER IN PRAISE OF WORK

Lord, today I went with a photographer to do a story on Living History Farms, an outdoor museum where the past is presented as truly as we can manage in the present.

The young woman at the 1840 farm was playing at being a pioneer farm wife, but her labor was real: hand-sewing a work shirt, stooping to weed her garden in a sunbonnet, cooking over an open fire. Her days are long and arduous, but at night she returns to electric lights, television, and running water.

At the 1900 farm, the youthful man and wife shelled corn with a hand-turned crank, racing to finish before the new harvest was brought to the cribs. They had been up since five o'clock, but they worked with unflagging energy.

The risks are not great for these young people. If their crops fail, they will continue to eat. If babies are born, there will be hospitals and doctors. Therefore, their serious play brings deep satisfaction. Their eyes are clear and unworried, and hard work brings them joy.

Am I not just as safe in Your hands in my own time? Safe enough to feel that my work is play? Thank You, Lord, for work and all its pleasures. Amen.

PRAYER FOR SOLVENCY

Father, this stack of bills terrifies me. I've never seen so many in one month—car repairs, new tires, gasoline, wedding presents, taxes, baby presents—and just after I wrote a check for the basic expenses of a college student whose back was to the wall.

I ordered a new kitchen window months ago. Please don't let it come until I can pay for it. I ordered one hundred copies of my published novel. Please let them arrive at the usual molasses pace.

And here's a letter from the young couple I help a little each month in their campus ministry. They have a new baby, and their support money must stretch accordingly. They ask me to pray about increasing my monthly check.

We have never been in debt, but that condition looks probable to me now. My part-time efforts just don't add up—at least not financially.

Even so, I grab the self-addressed card from the campus ministry couple and scribble, "Yes!" Please help me keep that promise. Amen.

PRAYER FOR THE FIRST DAY OF CLASSES

Still wearing a summer tan in place of stockings, I'm a teacher again, Lord. You made these twenty-three young people who offer computer cards to prove they have paid to learn. Help me to give them their money's worth.

This class is so much larger than my last—good news for the college business office, but a lot more papers for me to correct. Give me the energy to spread knowledge farther but not thinner.

Lord, give me the grace to maintain my standards lovingly, as You do. Sharpen my memory of my own beginnings and give me patience.

I thank You for these students. Help me to discover their good qualities quickly and to be charitable about their faults. You have made each of them beautiful in a special way, and I pray for the perception to find Your praiseworthy handiwork in them all.

Forgive me for my reluctance to meet this challenge after a summer too swiftly flown. Amen.

A YARD WOMAN'S PRAYER

It's dry, Lord, no rain for a month. When I prayed for time and breathing space, did You answer by removing the necessity of mowing the lawn? Now I'm praying that You'll give my poor, brown grass a drink.

I thank You for the beautiful oak tree that seeded itself in such a perfect spot at the edge of the lawn. So many seedlings have cracked the house foundation or sprouted in the driveway, but You placed this one at a break between the hydrangeas with room to grow and shade us from the setting sun.

I marvel at the beauty of the weeds You have created, so full of life and aglow with intricate blossoms. I pulled them until blistered fingers reminded me to save some to admire. My favorites are the clusters of tiny, white blooms that look like fireworks brought low. Your loving attention to detail in the weeds is a signpost to Your greater love made flesh in Christ.

Forgive me for resenting the time it takes to tend the jungle of my yard. I'm thankful for a plot of ground to call my own, which is more than my Lord Jesus had. Amen.

PRAYER FOR
A SICK EDITOR

My editor at the newspaper is in the hospital, Lord, and I realize that You knew it before I did. If it be Your will, dissolve the kidney stone and send him back to us.

I know that I complain about him, but I'm used to him, Lord, and I don't work as well for anyone else. Today it took me an hour to force myself to sit down and write a feature story—an hour of nonessential phone calls, pencil sharpening and desk arranging. I am accountable to him, and no one else cares as much. But I am accountable to You, too, and I want to be "a workman that needeth not to be ashamed".

How selfish I am to ask it this way! He has pain, and I'm sorry for that. His wife and children are worried, and I feel for them. Forgive my self-concern and accept my petition for better reasons.

Bless those whose burdens are heavier in his absence. Amen.

A HOUSEKEEPER'S PRAYER

Lord, my house is a mess, but I have deadlines to meet and papers to correct. If cleanliness is next to Godliness, I cannot face You.

The dining room table is piled high with papers and books. The carpet is covered with dog hair. The cat has thrown his soggy food on the kitchen floor. The breakfast dishes are in the sink. The laundry waits. How can my husband come home to this from his elegant, well-kept office?

Have I taken on too much? I seem to be a poor juggler, dropping two oranges to catch a third. Help me to set priorities sensibly, Lord, and on this day when I'm stuck, help me to take heart and begin—anything.

The deadlines must be met and the papers must be corrected, but the washer can run while I do one or the other. If I'm not tempted to browse, the dining-room table can be cleared in a hurry. I leave the rest in Your hands. Just give me the will to begin. Amen.

PRAYER FOR
A SON

The semester is not old enough for me to match all names and faces, Lord, and now my son phones to say that he is having matching trouble too, but of another kind.

The course he's complaining about is something dealing with mystical education, and he says, "The professor's head and mine are not in the same place. I don't know what's going on!" He fears academic disaster and is convinced that he will not be accepted by the law school—all because of mystical education.

A friend of mine steered him to the course, so I am ultimately responsible for his desperate situation. I called my friend immediately, and she says the professor is a good and deeply kind man who wants his students to find their own way.

Remind me that my son is an adult, Lord. Prevent me from swooping down on his problems as if he were a pre-schooler. You know how it hurts me to have him unhappy, but You also know what he needs for growth. Uphold him, help him to find his way, and keep me from interfering unprofitably. Amen.

PRAYER FOR
A VERY OLD POET

I interviewed an amazing child of Yours today, Lord. Her name is Olivia, and she knows You well. She told me that she does not suffer from the usual wakefulness of the aged but falls asleep immediately after saying her prayers.

"I don't believe very much in being dead," she said. "I love living!" Oh God, I thank You for the challenging zest of this woman. Olivia is almost blind, she suffers from arthritis, and she walks with a cane, but she praises life.

Thank You for the sight that I take for granted, for the books I can read, and for the faces and scenes I can see. Day after day, I run through my life, forgetting to be glad that I can without cane or pain.

Olivia was born in a log cabin. She weighed a pound and a half, and a feather pillow on hot bricks was her cradle. Her mother fed her with an eyedropper until she had a firm grip on life.

She was eighty-six when she wrote her first poem. Someone typed it for her, as has been done with the rest of her work. She can't see, but she can recite all of her work.

I thank You for Olivia, Lord; she is one of Your miracles. Help me to rise in the morning with one of her lines on my lips: "Press onward, be on your way. This may be your crowning day!" Amen.

PRAYER FOR A COLLEAGUE

Father, You know all about academic politics. Teaching so few hours at the college, I never expected to be touched by them, but now I am.

My friend Marcella is fighting for principle in a hiring matter, believing in a cause that seems incomprehensible to many. She suffers.

Today she invited me to lunch in the faculty dining room. We were the only women present, and men I had believed to be my friends studied their plates diligently as we passed their tables or muttered a choked "hello".

I am angry for Marcella's sake, Father. Help me to rise above my contempt for this kind of behavior and do something positive to help her. Help me to realize that some of these cowards are hostages to fortune. They have wives and children who cannot be nourished on support for an unpopular cause. I thank You that I am free to speak for the right as I see it, and I ask that You will give me clear vision to that end. And Lord, make Marcella strong, for she has much to bear. Amen.

PRAYER IN
PRAISE OF MUSIC

Lord, I reviewed the Chicago Symphony Orchestra last night, and my spirit soared right through the ceiling of the concert hall, singing to You, the Maker of these magnificent musicians.

And yet, when I asked one of them, "What makes the Chicago Symphony the great instrument that it is? What's the secret?", he answered, "We work like hell!"

I understood what he meant, because all art and every worthy outcome depends on hard and persistent effort, but his answer melted the wax on my wings. Working like hell, taken literally, means unending exertion with no results: Sisyphus pushing his stone uphill eternally.

The man plays like an angel but speaks like a mortal, creating perfect music and flawed speech. I praise You for the magnificent intonation, virtuosity and sensitive musicianship of the Chicago Orchestra instrumentalists, and I also praise You for the energy and motivation that makes them "work like hell". I praise You for transforming grubby, exhausting practice that calls forth such a baneful description into the celestial sound that lifts the soul. Amen.

PRAYER OF THANKS

Father, I thank You for the long-awaited rain. The shiny streets, the dripping branches, and even the wet dogs confined to the basement are a deep joy after the dry, dusty weeks that threatened the death of every growing thing. The drought went on for so long that I would have been afraid if I hadn't believed in Your goodness.

The grass that seemed so dead two days ago is reviving, greening delicately through the brown stubble. Drooping stems are straightening miraculously, and leaves in the early stages of withering have regained their true shapes. What a glad resurrection!

Father, I pray for the farmers for whom the gift of rain arrived too late. Help them to look ahead to another better harvest with hope.

This soft, gray day is so beautiful to me, and I am filled with praise and thankfulness. I will dry the dogs with a towel so they can come upstairs and be glad with me. Amen.

PRAYER FOR FORBEARANCE

Lord, somebody broke twenty-one windows in our church last night. The news gave me a cold feeling in the pit of my stomach, then a hot flare of rage. Who would dare to despoil the house of the Lord? Their capture and punishment obsessed me.

From the pulpit, our pastor said, "The gut reaction is to catch whoever did it and punch them, but we must ask ourselves what condition a person would have to be in to do such a thing. We must deal with this redemptively."

Oh Lord, why are our most Christian thoughts so often second thoughts? Of course we must feel sympathy for the emptiness that expresses itself in senseless destruction.

The vandal (there could be more than one) needs redemption and the capacity for love it brings, but we do not know where to carry the Good News. You know, Lord. Hear our prayers for the destroyer(s) and lead him, her, or them to know Your Son. Amen

PRAYER FOR PATIENCE

The editor of the student newspaper is in my class, Lord, and he asked me to do a critique of the paper during a class session. I have avoided this for years, never even mentioning the name of the publication, because I don't want to be its faculty adviser.

I couldn't resist the editor's request, and so it began—the tearing down with all the students jumping in. We talked about the bumping headlines, the dull leads, the typographical errors, and the cloying cuteness of the content. Suddenly, I recognized my own cruelty and searched for something good to say. I could find very little, but the editor perceived my fumbling attempt, and that made the harsh comments easier to bear. Oh God, help me to find the good things first to cushion the critical things that must be said.

Now my heart is full of thanks because we criticized another issue and there have been improvements. Not many, but enough to give me hope. Today, You helped me say the good things first. Amen.

PRAYER FOR COMFORT

Father, I am hurt beyond tears. You know how hard I worked on that novel—the months of research, the intensity of the writing that went on for nearly a year. Today it came back to me with a form rejection letter.

Are You teaching me patience? I know about the tribulation that worketh patience, experience, hope, and joy, and if that is what this is all about, I must accept the situation without self-pity. But it's hard, Father, so very hard! There are courses in speed reading and speed writing; there are instant photographs, instant potatoes, and instant coffee, but not, I suppose, instant patience.

I know You love me and that You are at the helm of my life, and yet I complain. Forgive me for that. I am down, so far down that I'm in the dark, Lord. Help me up and give me light. May I not whine to my dear ones about this defeat, causing them sorrow. I thank You for the warm acceptance *they* always give me.

About the manuscript—You know the desire of my heart. If it accords with Your shaping of my life, please let it find a home sometime. Amen.

PRAYER FOR
A DAUGHTER AND HER
HUSBAND

Father, how good it was to have our first-born back again for a few days! She and I went shopping, sat at the table and talked for hours, and just enjoyed looking at each other while her seminarian husband worked on a sermon upstairs.

He is happy, confident that he is in Your will, and the only thing that clouds his joy is her restlessness. She prepared herself to teach, but there are no teaching jobs in the seminary town. We are grieved that she must take a job below her qualifications, but we are trying to help by financing her graduate work in another discipline.

At least she loves You and knows that her destiny is in Your hands. Uphold her, Father, and lift the burden of her discontent from the young husband we love as one of our own.

I thank You for the two of them and for this time we have had together. Help them to serve You mightily and with joy. Amen.

PRAYER FOR MY HUSBAND

Lord, so often I thank You for guiding my choice of a mate. I was too young to choose well on my own, and Your goodness alone is responsible for our enduring partnership.

As a lawyer, he bears the burdens of others, but he never brings them home to me. From the first, he spent time with our children and was fully present with them. When they played games, he never let them win because they were little. While they joked that every game was "Daddy wins," they finally had the pure joy of winning a few by their own skill.

When I am sad or sick, he gets angry, but I finally know how to take that as his expression of love. And sometimes when we have a rare evening at home, a time to read, he looks up from his book. I feel his gaze, look up from my own book and hear him say, "I've always been glad that I married you." My faltering "Me too!" is inadequate, but he knows and You know how grateful I am.

Take care of him, keep him well, and give him strength for his work and our life. Amen.

SECOND PRAYER FOR PATIENCE

Father, most of my accomplishments are solo efforts, and You know how hard it is for me to work with a committee. Help me truly to love my neighbor as myself, to empathize to the point where I feel her uncertainties, her need for prolonged discussion of a matter that seems cut and dried to me.

Remind me, Father, that the working out of Your purpose in history has been a long, long process with many byways, and that little of it has been accomplished by impatient loners.

Keep me from drumming my fingers, from calling the question too abruptly, and from voicing exasperation about the slow business of coming to a meeting of minds. Above all, do not let me abandon cooperative effort.

I thank You for people of good will who come together to accomplish a good work. Bless all committees that are in Your will and smooth their paths. Amen.

OCTOBER PRAYER

Dear Lord, I glory in Your October world! The sky is an almost painfully beautiful blue, the maples blaze red and orange, and the oak leaves are curls of maroon and russet. The fall roses have a deeper fragrance than the blooms of summer, and the stars shine with a sharper light in the autumn sky.

Like the year, I am no longer young, Lord, but I thank You for bringing me this far. Many of the uncertainties of my earlier years are gone, and You have helped me to find my path and given me strength to follow it.

I have a sense of my own mortality, but I am not afraid, because eternal life is mine, here and now, as well as when You call me home.

So let me blaze like the leaves, give fragrance like the rose, and shine like the autumn stars. When my season here is done, I will live again in the springtime of Your presence. Amen.

PRAYER FOR MY MOTHER

Father, I thank You for my mother and for her unfailing acceptance of me no matter how much I have failed. She is old now and sick, but still full of spirit.

I see in her a deep anger that she cannot control her world, and I pray that You will remind her that You can and do—all is well.

"I am good for nothing!" she complains, but that is not so. She prays unceasingly for all of us, she visits the sick, and she encourages the disheartened. Show her the value of what she does, Lord.

Her life has been a litany of sorrows and frustrations, Father, but she has borne them with patience. Even now, as her body fails her, she smiles and says, "Everything wears out eventually!" Still, Father, I know that she rages against the dying of the light. Be merciful to her in her infirmities and illumine her with Your own light. Amen.

PRAYER FOR OUR PETS

Father, I thank You for the animals that warm our lives: for Kuki, the Siamese, who purrs on my lap and puts his sable paws around my neck like loving arms; for Alex, the Afghan hound who has been with us from puppyhood to gray-bearded wisdom; and for Sheba, our younger Afghan, so insecure and flighty with others but so loving toward us.

They are beautiful, Father, so graceful and marvelously formed in colors from palest cream and tawny apricot to rich brown and black. At rest or in motion, they are a reminder to praise Your creation.

When we take them to the kennel before a trip, the house is empty and forlorn without them. They are so much a part of our lives, drawing our concern and offering theirs, giving us exercise and companionship.

I want to believe that heaven will include dogs and cats, Lord, but most theologians do not encourage my hope. They only say that nothing necessary for happiness will be lacking. I'll hold onto my hope, and in the meantime, bless my beasts. Amen.

PRAYER FOR FORGIVENESS

Lord, the piano tuner is working downstairs. He strikes insistently, and there is dissonance. It occurs to me that I, myself, need tuning.

I have been hurried, harried, preoccupied, and not at all in tune with the needs of others. A friend has problems, but I have no time to listen. Forgive me for that. When someone causes me inconvenience, I scowl and snap without considering the possibility of extenuating circumstances. Forgive me for that, too. I rush through my daily Bible reading with unseeing eyes, too hurried to let the meaning in. Forgive me, Lord.

"I have no time!" I say, but that is not true. You give me twenty-four hours in a day, the same span You give to everyone else, but the tension of my strings is wrong. I need tuning. I have waited too long before asking You to correct my pitch, but I ask it now. Amen.

PRAYER FOR
A FAMOUS AUTHOR

Father, Isaac Bashevis Singer came to town today, and I asked the paper to send me to do the interview. I discovered Singer's rich, fictional world years ago and have since admired the energy and joy of his creation.

He calls You a novelist and the Old Testament episodes in the Divine Novel. He says Your wastebasket is filled with unsuccessful work. If You have such a wastebasket, Lord, it is filled with those who throw themselves into it by the free will that Singer acknowledges as Your gift.

He may be right about the Divine Novel analogy, but I wish he would read on into the great pages of the New Testament and pick up the greatest story ever told. Singer still waits for the Messiah, more with wry endurance than with hope.

"There is a God," he said, "but He never reveals Himself. No one knows His purpose."

I commit I. B. Singer to You, Lord. Show him Your purpose and let him presume on Your acquaintance as I do with such grateful love. Amen.

NOVEMBER PRAYER

The leaves are dead, blowing about in a strong wind, but the sun is warm. In this brief lull before the winter, I washed windows and raked, wishing I had enough time to finish both jobs properly. But I took time to sit in the sun and read.

My life is like that, Lord. It has warm days when I might prepare for the cold ahead, but I never seem to have time to put myself in order. Instead, I try to prolong the warmth and pretend it will last; then I must face my inner winter with dirty windows and ungathered leaves.

Be with me in all seasons, Father. Help me to store the satisfactions of an undemanding day to help me through the hectic times. Give me the time and the determination to wash all the windows of my soul without leaving streaks and to rake together the leaves of obligation and put them where they belong. Amen.

PRAYER FOR THOSE WHO HAVE GONE BEFORE

Father, today my friend and I visited Bishop Hill, the Swedish religious colony founded in 1846. I had been there many times before, but Bishop Hill is different now.

Many of the old brick buildings are restored, a cheery restaurant serves Swedish food, and gift shops sell bright and appealing Swedish imports.

Behind this charming mask is the pain of the first settlers, who were persecuted for their beliefs in Sweden and suffered in different ways in their New Jerusalem. Beatings and stonings in Sweden were exchanged for hunger, cold, disease, and death in America.

The people put their trust in one man, their prophet, and he was murdered. They expected him to rise again on the third day like our Lord, and when he did not, they had to revise their faith.

Father, I thank You for those staunch, true-hearted Swedes who served You with all their might according to their lights. They were faithful to their purpose, which they thought was Yours, and may that testimony shine through the ages. Amen.

PRAYER OF THANKSGIVING

Dear Lord, only a nation that suspects it is insufficiently thankful for an uncommon number of blessings would proclaim a special day for giving thanks. That day is tomorrow, but I hope that I am just as thankful today or any other day.

Is it smug to count the ways You have blessed me and mine? Each morning I thank you for life, for love, for the awesome intricacy of Your creation, for work to do, and most especially for Your Son.

Our former pastor used to thank You every Sunday for "leaving no visible marks of Your displeasure" upon our little flock, even when *I* thought those marks were plain to see. I now believe that You never punish us, and that what I once viewed as punishment is really child training, lessons taught by a loving Father.

And so I am thankful, not *for* all things, but *in* all things, knowing that all things work together for good in Your plan for me. This, above all, is my cause for thanksgiving, but I also thank You for health, comfort, and the zest to find life good. Amen.

A PRAYER FOR MENDING

Father, the tile man is working in my bathroom, pounding and scraping. I helped him until I cut my hand and bled too much to continue.

Those tiles must be thirty years old, and we can't match their color or size, so we must remove them from the sagging plaster carefully and re-affix them to a new wall.

How much easier it would be to pry them off roughly and replace them with new ones. But they are beautiful and worth saving. Their quality has not been seen for years.

So it is with our lives. When a relationship begins to sag, we may be too busy and impatient to mend it, or we may not be willing to cut our hands on the sharp grout of an association that is coming apart.

You know the old friend I'm thinking of, Lord, and You know the shame I feel about our misunderstanding. Help me to put a new wall behind that lovely old tile and to say the mending words. Amen.

PRAYER FOR
A NEW SEASON

Father, the shock of the first heavy snow has us reeling. That heavy white mantle is Your gift, but it frightens us, and we must learn quickly to drive in another way and to dress differently.

I must travel slippery streets to teach my class and to interview my subjects, and I consciously put myself in Your hands each time I set out. Not that I think of You less on a fine, warm day, but I depend on You less completely then. Forgive me for behaving as if Christianity were a form of accident insurance.

I do thank You when, warm and safe inside my house, I look out at the snow-crowned pines and telephone wires that are white tracks to infinity. Your sleeping natural world lies quiet beneath the thick coverlet You provide, gathering strength for the time of waking. I hold my breath at its beauty—as a mother marvels at her sleeping child—and thank You for the eyes that let me see this winter picture.

When my blood grows thicker, Lord, I will thank You more for this new winter and shiver less in it. Bless and relieve those without warm houses and warm clothes and rescue those who quake in the winter of the soul. Amen.

ADVENT PRAYER

The first purple candle of Advent was lit at church today, Father, with the children repeating the glad foretelling of Christ's birth. This was a truly joyous moment of recognition, preceding the anxieties about material preparations for Christmas.

The Bible does not tell us that Mary, who knew the wondrous truth about her coming child, flew into a frenzy of buying and planning. Somehow, she had swaddling clothes when they were needed, but that was all.

Why, then, must we bake, buy, and wrap ourselves into short-tempered exhaustion as the weeks of the Advent season melt away? Oh Lord, help me to accomplish as much as is needful before my strength and good nature wear thin, and with the lighting of each purple candle, may I recapture the gladness I felt at the first tongue of flame in that wreath.

Keep me from a preoccupation with things as the season advances and remind me that Christmas gifts should include full attention, concern, and love. These were the gifts of Mary to her Son, and they were far more valuable than gold, frankincense, and myrrh. Amen.

PRAYER FOR MY STUDENTS

Father, with only three more classes left in the semester, many of my students are filled with anxiety. Until now, they believed they had forever to do make-up work, to do better. Some of them have done a poor job of numbering their days.

I am tempted to find an escape for those doomed to fail: something like extra assignments or turning a blind eye to their shortcomings. But if I do, they may gain a false impression of reality. Later, they may be careless when it counts, losing a job or ruining a relationship.

Father, I know that You take no pleasure in seeing us reap the consequences of wrong acts, but You do not rescue us, *deus ex machina*, because You want us to learn. Help me to remember this when I am tempted to rush to a sentimental rescue.

I pray for all my students, asking You to help them bear the tensions of exam week and to do their best. Be with them as they leave me and go on. Amen.

PRAYER OF
JOY

Father, You answered me so graciously when I prayed for clear roads to drive across the state to do a reading, and I thank You.

I met new people, all trying as earnestly to write successfully as I am, and they made me feel both welcome and special.

This was the big city of my childhood, the place where we went when our small town could not supply our needs, and I was so happy to return to it, hoping this time to give rather than take.

I read a little from my small body of published work and a lot from the unpublished to people of mixed ages who, though they were few in number, responded generously. Bless them in their own efforts, Lord.

After the program, a few of us talked for hours, and I think You gave me the right words to convince one young man that death is not "the ultimate," as he put it.

I do thank You for allowing me to be confirmed, if only briefly, by this appreciation of my writing efforts. Amen.

PRAYER AT
THE MANGER

Oh Lord, this long-awaited Holy Night is here, and I hold my breath in awe. My dear ones are safely gathered in and sleeping upstairs, the crumpled napkins and bits of cookies have been cleared away, and the cups and plates are washed after our annual Christmas Eve open house. The preparations for the family dinner tomorrow have been made.

Our adult children still hang their stockings for Santa Claus, and theirs are old and battered, veterans of many Christmases. Our son-in-law has a new one, as bright and beautiful as his presence among us.

I fill the stockings with little things they need or want—film, gum, a typewriter ribbon, dried figs, ballpoint pens, panty-hose, sweat socks, and popcorn balls. And then I sit beside the dying fire and read the wondrous story from Luke. Oh God, I am filled with adoration and gratitude beyond expression for the greatest Gift of all time.

I lock the doors and gaze for a moment at the painted Nativity scene in the yard before I turn off its spotlight. Oh, dearest Child! Then, when the house is dark except for the faint light from the hearth, I lift the ceramic Baby Jesus from the top of the television set and hold Him to my heart, feeling the Incarnation with my whole being. Thanks be to God! Amen.